Saint Agnes Outside the Walls

GEORGE MOORE

FUTURECYCLE PRESS

www.futurecycle.org

Library of Congress Control Number: 2016950789

Published by FutureCycle Press
Lexington, Kentucky, USA

ISBN 978-1-942371-05-2

For Tammy, my patron saint

Contents

I. Martyrs

The Order of Things...9
After Cavafy... 10
Café on the Alentejo... 11
The Unexpected Nature of Things....................................12
Gentle to Violent Rain... 13
Saint Agnes Outside the Walls... 14
Waiting Room.. 15
Note Saves Me from Despair.. 16
The Death of Modernism.. 18
Of Two Pietas.. 19
Translating Cavafy.. 20

II. Spanish for Tourists

Boat to Skellig Michael.. 23
At Skibbereen.. 24
The Swim to Iceland.. 25
A Skull on Orkney.. 26
Icelandic Time.. 28
How to Handle a Rattlesnake... 29
A Wild Grave... 30
Spanish for Tourists... 31
Tristan and Isolde.. 32
Sandstone House... 33

III. When in Rome

The Center of the Earth... 37
The Writer and His Horse... 38
Brennus and His Share of the Spoils (1893)....................... 39
Popular Culture... 40
The Dogs of Yucatán.. 41
Hadrian's Wall.. 42
After Celan... 43
The Gates of Hell.. 44

The Fall of Rome..46

Romulus and Remus.. 47

Saint Agnes, Outside... 48

IV. Illuminati

Adagio for Pen and Song...53

The Kennewick Man...54

Dwelling.. 55

Ode to the Clay Army, Xi'an, China...56

Chowder... 57

The Barbarians...58

Illuminati... 59

The South Cross... 60

Saint Agnes Returns to Rome..61

Schoenberg's Daughter's White Cat.. 62

The Unseen... 63

Belled Horses in a Portuguese Field.. 64

Capela Dos Ossos... 65

Birds of the Alentejo.. 66

V. Extinctions

Spanish Grave.. 69

Between Christmas and New Year's..70

How the World Works in Iceland.. 72

The Caper Berry..73

The Elgin Marbles.. 74

Extinctions... 75

Lightning.. 76

Why We Work with Our Hands..77

The Butcher's Table.. 78

Miss Havisham.. 79

I. Martyrs

"It's true that the human body is more vulnerable
than the products of the human mind."

—Salman Rushdie

"In order to understand, I destroyed myself."

—Fernando Pessoa, *The Book of Disquiet*

The Order of Things

In the days before temptations,
when the boys urged on by their

Everclear slip-drive madness
consumed everything in their path,

I escaped to here, poet nested
amid disorders, a post-holocaust

Hamlet, his final failure to remain
detached from that which he hates.

For me it was love. Liberal sprinkling
vs. deep ecology. Somewhere

in-between, where natural wonder,
after an anxiety of influences,

pushes you to a decision, all
poppycock or ague,

dumdum fever, zaniness, but real
as Alzheimer's, you recognize

the graying mass about the center of things,
begin to see how you have distributed

the pro/con forces of your life.
Poets take a second name, parted

right down the middle. I'd give anything
to return: a bottle on the waves,

a message in bad grammar, to flit
through dreams of things not said

but dreamed of saying, to that love
made milky like ouzo, the untested time

accepted in theories of the universal,
when we spoke gibberish, turned chaos

into a chant, assuring ourselves
that this was but the order of things.

After Cavafy

There is, of course, in each of us
this Greek god, this mad desire for love
with a world that does not respond.

What have you heard of the others,
burned alive or beaten to death for love?
They are not martyrs, but magicians

cured of their fears by human crowds.
What was the last thing you heard: love
is only a word? The seas will drown

such blasphemies, the gods rise up
and wipe the earth clean of this false love
that does not know right from wrong.

Café on the Alentejo

Coffee for the poor
is heart's blood,
the oil that runs the body's machinery,
a dark sun on the crest of an inner landscape
at morning's break point
with the sea of the night.

Without cafés along the *praça*
where would people congregate
outside of churches
to talk of the gods
in milder manners
or peel back the new work day?

Without this ebony sea of marrow
there'd be trouble in the land of sheep.
Without love in this dark drop of blood,
the bean of the universe
with its broken energies,
night rays imagined in the day's core,

hours would pass, surely,
but without relief. And in this
condensed moment of Alentejo time
there would be no tongues of Portuguese,
nor the slow crescendoing European,
but merely the static echoes of history.

Without this demitasse of ardor
and amperage, no one would hear the bells
as the cattle drop their heads to feed,
no one would speak of their poverty,
or of their hours, newly blessed,
with the mud of the earth in their veins.

The Unexpected Nature of Things

Not all things of course. Not
the way a Portuguese horse will bow its head
to fill its belly with grass, ringing its collar bell.

Not the radiation from the sun
when your skin signals a movement of clouds
and your eyes are perfectly closed.

Not standing still at a furious rate of speed
in the middle of a crowd, in a silence
that you feed on like a chick its shell.

But how a cup of tea on the table at the lip
of sun and umbrella shadow can retrieve
a memory, and revive the dead.

Gentle to Violent Rain

Beneath the grand umbrellas
on Paroikia's small square, the rain at first
no more than a May interruption, an island
hesitation, Mediterranean storms with sprinkling,
votive gestures, the slate walks wetting
slowly, turning dark gray.

Then the rivulets running off
the umbrellas, bouncing in drops from eaves,
racing across the wood soffit, finding
the marble tops of tables, the demitasse,
the glass of water, as if the water
were an ancient twin.

And close to you now, moved
by the falling spray, sharing the last dry
edge of outdoor cushion, others having
run inside the cafés, squeezed into a space
both sacred and profane, the rain
releases us to the first

hintings of desire, to the warmth
of body hemisphere, planetary turbulence
of this Greek isle, this walkway café,
our other lives like satellites, forgotten
on the outer rims of experience
for an afternoon, under water.

Saint Agnes Outside the Walls

If you mention Rome, the girl
on a particular night, the café,
of course, a cappuccino as only
Rome can imagine, swirl of cream
in the impending darkness,
what name do you give her?

At twenty there was all the world
before you. Now there is history,
a dull spark at the back of the skull.

But at thirteen she is gone.
What name do you carve on these walls,
in the catacombs beneath her grave?

The girl at the table across the patio
smiles. It is night and the café is full,
and the light from the streets
makes a catacomb of the stones.

If you think back to the moment,
then it is a passage back,
a way through. To martyr oneself
at such an age. The night unsexed
with electric lights.

There is nothing to do but wait.
The café has emptied, the crowds
dispersed, faces slowly ebbing away.
The girl whose name you remember
as Agnes, in a Rome of which
not a stone remains.

Waiting Room

After all that time, I was out of the room.
The breath rose up and evaporated in a black sun.

That's what the poem wants, some kind of immediacy.
But then death comes out of nowhere, always.

Going going gone. The life I did not see coming,
did not see the meaning of, the weight of, escapes even

as it has arrived. Now the idea of death is the providence
of the poem, the brief conclusion that goes nowhere,

yet it cannot quite reach back either. For this man
it was no postmodern decay, no great tabooed mania

of cells, but only old age, an empty cellar, a phone ringing
at the end of an empty hall. He taught me how

a doctor views the changes toward death. The hospital
cares less. They milk the cattle, no matter how

humanitarian the dream. So the poem must become
more than what is actually said. This is the room

where the poem lives, where he was breathing. This space
that does not live and never has, but speaks of living.

The poem separates itself and dies on the page.
And only the living can revive it. It crawls back into me.

He said a hundred times that he was ready to go.
That is what he said. The poem is proof we were ready.

It does not matter that the room was empty in the end.
After years, all this time spent making a single day.

Note Saves Me from Despair

It is Saturday and I am reading Jack Spicer,
so goes this wandering, as long as
it leaves the moon in its deep hole,

but more, I am reading the *Collected Poems*,
collected because he is dead.
What a time to be lamenting the word

as the start of a relationship that lives
in the past, and thinking of San Francisco
in the early 1960s, and how every tercet

would have failed, like the three flags
of another country where only seniors
are poets playing with their pensions,

and lamenting the fall of the great line,
fearing the never-to-be recovery of poems
on the beach, the shipwreck of space

and time. This far into the murky reality
of the future, I see Jack as a kind of mild
madman, believing in love and himself

only secondly, and then questioning
what the self could do on a Saturday afternoon
without a car or a sunny day to steer it,

and it makes no difference that I am here
on the cold shore of Nova Scotia
on another planet, wishing poetry would

fly me out of the self again, lift me
like a magic carpet, lilting in the wind
of a line, a turn of surreal phrase,

forever to not care about the future,
or the college students staring, or a girl
whose reality became simply a name,

drowned, and I come across a wide-lined
slip of paper, folded so flat it must be
forty years old, hidden in the center of Jack's

laments about the distance he is from
friends, that summer in San Francisco,
and how poetry which was so meant

to save him keeps sadly slipping away,
and read a list of key figures through
history, or histories we might say today,

Aquinas, Rimbaud, the Republic of Plato,
Buddha, Chaucer, Jean of Arc, with dates
next to their names, and wonder

if the tercet will survive the Flood,
if after we've come and gone our distances
increase or disappear, and if we become

like slips of forgotten wide-lined
notebook paper, always meaningful,
always carrying the wound of the personal

like a foreign flag into some country
where everyone has waited for spring
even through the long months of summer.

The Death of Modernism

For Carter, wherever he is

The very last time, in the library,
you had thrown your shoes away
saying it was spring,
you wouldn't be needing them.

The streets safer than before
violence brewed on ill-lit screens,
and in neighborhood divorces
and dark centers

of disremembered cities. A game,
living, not just the aftercrop of philosophy.
In high school, we knew each other
indifferently, mad at the edges,

wanting something to break through to.
Trailing rain, you wandered into
the Denver Public Library
in ragged sweater and threadbare jeans.

I was hunting the history of something
for a paper due the next day—the concrete
path already darkening with rain—
without exoneration.

You there at the edge of things,
always ready for the next thing
in a perpetual day, the wave of the world,
for a moment, holding you up,

until you slipped out, praising
the rain, without a place we could agree on,
the library an aquarium, a joke
housing the drowned.

Of Two Pietas

That year in Florence, a moving walkway
carried me past mother and child,
the mother bent over her fallen child,
much as the time a walkway carried me

past Lenin's tomb on Red Square.
But there, everyone asked, *Is he real
or wax to look so perfectly preserved?*
How odd that moving walkways

move us so. What sorrows migrate
through a poet's mind, like birds of different
species gathering together, or lovers,
times cross and confess in the same way.

Before the Pieta, bulletproof glass,
her fragile features spray-painted once,
another time, smashed with a hammer.
The iconoclast himself a child of the times.

Now, having lost her innocence,
she achieves a fragile equilibrium, art
and artifact as one, love grafted on an act
of violence. Her complexion turned to stone.

But then, I've known beauty in another world.
A local figure, carved of wood, rode the shoulders
of working men through the streets of Cuzco,
her darker skin truer to the origins, her red dress

catching fire in the sun. Younger then,
what is it I remember? Her features were
like a stir of milk and blood, black beads
completed with gold brocade, and she was

carried church to church, and rode a rough pallet
on bare shoulders. Two sisters of the sorrows;
martyrs, their sons. One cut of polished stone,
the other made of wood, the natural capital of fire.

Translating Cavafy

On Rhodes, I thought to translate you
but knew no Greek, only *Kaliméra,*
Kalispéra, feeling alienated

from the poet in me. I longed
to look into the eyes of someone
to see history—but that was wrong.

It was history you were given
by someone you longed for. An island
library was run by a young man

not unlike one of your gods,
disguised. He said he'd help me
with derivations. But that was

as far as we got. The Rhodes' sun
that May was unusually hot, but
there are eleven shadowy gates

and a moat transformed into a garden
that make good walks in the evenings,
and all I could want of a way

to waste time. I wrote of cats and cafés,
as everyone does, but could not
translate a word. Everything

came in on a wave and dissolved
into the present. We heard Alexandria
was shelled after you left, and fire

destroyed the place you lived.
It seems the gods have no favorites.
They abandon the living and the dead.

II. Spanish for Tourists

"It was impossible to imagine these hills giving forth anything but the soft syllables of Irish, just as only certain forms of German could be spoken on the high crags of Europe; or Dutch in the muddy, guttural, phlegmish lowlands."

—Alexander McCall Smith, *Portuguese Irregular Verbs*

Boat to Skellig Michael

Like the monks, we make pilgrimages
everywhere we go. Today, it's to the rocks
off the coast, out of the inlet from Portmagee,
the sea here famous and forgotten.
No more than a boat or two heads out.

Slate dull waves front the trawler's hull
in chants and rhythms. Or is it simply the quiet
that accentuates the silences tangled in the depths
among us? The journey only an hour or two,
far less than for the monks of the ninth century.

Once or twice a year, the hermits returned to shore.
But the rock was their element of faith,
a flourish of gannets their worst temptation, and six
hundred slate steps, a fortress, a wind-challenged
steep of meditations. Salt air whipped to holy fire.

Their beehive huts little more than caves.
I have to ask, what kind of god confused life
and death? Yet we climb today like penitents,
but without their certainty in the future.
When the mist rises, we can see the mainland.

The more they looked to escape this world,
the more the world sought them out as saints.
Their wisdom was not a word but wind.
Today, the gannets soil the rock;
the men must have done the same.

When Vikings finally came to plunder,
their gods fiercer than the wounded *Passion,*
more fire and fury than cold sea and rock,
the hermits simply sailed off the edge of the earth
in search of another heaven.

At Skibbereen

At Skibbereen, I run with the cows,
a free man. They gather near the slow garden of the sea,
crowd the narrow lane down to the next field,
always their destination, and brush the gate
pressing in toward the grain trough.

That there was ever bred a creature like this,
burnt chocolate as bog, without a care but to feed,
clopping in thunder along the tarmac road,
wallowing toward some vague sense of home,
even as we do. I rise up

past drystone fences, smelling
the sea and manure, something in the morning
sweet, indiscernible, but not rotted,
blooming, transforming
the sluggish morning's reverie.

With these Kerry cows, I crest the hill
that leads to Roaringwater Bay
but cannot run so far,
while ancient vines reach out and caress my face.
This late sympathy with the slowness of life,

no wind, and sun just touching hedgerow,
wraps me in the lifting mist,
fine as a solitary thought, transient and real,
and I turn to descend the road again,
remembering.

The Swim to Iceland

We drive along the coastal road a day
or perhaps only a moment after the polar bear
lumbered down the same uneven road.
Riding the ice from Greenland,

floating and swimming, and what was it
she was looking for, was she lost or was it
some urge to see the edge of the world,
as it's dwindling? Of course, when she arrives

she's shot and killed. This is the new world,
after all, island headlands of the Pole, too small
and crowded for her kind, too computerized
and full of thermal swimming pools.

If only the bears could shrink
as the polar ice cap does, *dissolve into a dew?*
But like Hamlet they are too physical,
too much of this world.

White as a flag on this greening coast,
white as sky but air alone cannot hide her,
and the whiteness now does not stay all summer.
The hunt happens almost immediately.

She cannot reach the interior. Lost there,
she might emerge anywhere into the cities,
such as they are, hard miles from the ice fields.
One bear, more or less, and death

is but a sign of the times. One lumbering
mammal up from the frozen sea, stood erect
and watched her ice sheet breaking up, before
she crossed the aberrant green.

A Skull on Orkney

I watch the others
hand the skull around
like a paperweight,
hefting human history
in their thoughts
like a stone.

I let my turn pass.
The artifact moves
in another circle
around the equinox,
shadowing a life
impossible to know.

Hamlet's cue
to enquire of mortality,
the *Tomb of Eagles*
falls short of its own
question: How does
death interpret for us?

How such a thing
stripped of its flesh
can come back into
the heart. The eager
mind has little
hesitation.

Surely life on Orkney
was a life of struggle,
each burial adding
to the grave, each
one born a prisoner
of the sea.

I'm not skittish
in the face of death
I let it pass by me:
dead tokens of men
in curious hands.
But better to be buried

in a stone cairn
rather than hefted
around each morning
in the thin sun, among
rude silences, in
living awe.

Icelandic Time

These mulls of an island north enough to freeze deep
as when the earth first formed, was flooded, and stones rose

to meet a burning sky, are battled by breaths of chill air
as we cross the tundra between glaciovolcanoes. Rock

seems suspended in both time and space, in clocks of peat
and bogs, and then the sudden ashen sawdust covers

everything. It was three generations after the events of 1783
before the ground regained its fledgling fields, potatoes

the size of a child's fist, and anemic carrots. Time here
is layers of slag or dross, all things built up into lava skirts,

an alibi of ages, with remains of geophysical exertions,
and planetary motions that stay frozen in the ice. Time waits

in the first fissure again, nested in the shadows that precede
seasons, the dark of winter like a birth canal, then, spring's

effusive babbling. All traditions at their birth are geologic.
So we assume, on this tundra, that Viking DNA was mined

in the ages when life was an unsettling of early settlements.
Bloodwise, all teleseismic activity is an echo of the human.

We use time's language to build new energies like water
beading up on black rock in older dialects of iron and basalt.

So when someone says *Já*, we hear the spear-end of *Icelander.*
One eye always looking north, the other becomes an island

on the face of the Earth, seeing before we see, staring
into the cold while squinting at a fixed and tireless sun.

How to Handle a Rattlesnake

Gently, with a reverence for the long history laid out before you.
Reach only so far as you can yourself strike. Extend your body
outward, into the universe. Remember the hunger that knows only itself.
Evolve away from words into a world before their hollow was filled.
Carry a pail with a lid that does not fit tightly,
carry it through tall grass and over naked, rocky terrain.
Speak then of your feat without exaggeration. Confess
to the poison of myth, to a belief in dangling ropes,
to all the other realities that circle the world. See the thin trail
you share now in a momentary liquid of time. Watch
where you step. Catching is easier than letting go.

A Wild Grave

The grave is quickly overgrown.
Even the small trees planted on you
are consumed in the furious undergrowth
of Canada thistle and milkweed and loam.
And the path down to you, no longer a path
but a hedged-in tunnel of weeds and grass.
Time envelopes the lines of your last place,
but the earth continues to grow. Nature's
relentless attitude is a nonchalance
that buries us and brings us back again.
The pumps of the universe, the blood cells
of cycles that release you into the world,
pound through the still spring air. The ants
are mad as fire while furious gnats take up
a perpetual dance. I catch you in a crown
of seeded grass, at the corner of my eye,
that last look before you turn and bolt and
disappear into the breathing wilds.

Spanish for Tourists

This Spanish comes from the mouth,
not from those skinny books I brought.
Who has time for books? I witness

las turists, the herd, but then I am
among them, of them, inescapably.
What is more foreign than the I of this

other world? *¿Cuánto debo?* What
is it I owe you? You who know
the language of the ancient Conquests?

Not a colloquy of the islands,
but the pure quetzal flutterings of speech
found under dark archways

in the Governor's Palace, Uxmal,
that language that could only be shared
with one you had to become.

It's the *me olvidé*, the *I forgot.* This
Spanish is rain and jungle heat, *sapote*,
the chocolate fruit, verbs cast in shadows

of straw fedoras on dark faces. Parrot fish
off Garrafón are its forgotten tongue,
lost to *la tourista.* The cameras snap

indelible greens bleached by the Gulf
to unbelievable. I desire that other
within you, *quiero quedar otra*,

the *cenoté*, well of the night, pure sound
filling my absence, staying with me
till morning in that never foreign place,

forgotten, or only just beginning to be
remembered, opening again,
the luxuriant flora of your first word.

Tristan and Isolde

Now, it is the old man's turn.
He's no longer a king, nor of notable fame.
But his understanding places him
beyond the warring tribes of younger men.
He knows what a woman sees, and more,
how to temper his own desires.
He gives himself up to her imaginings.
The passion of young men cannot last;
it is a passion for ships at sea, for potions,
for the mind's ability to master games.
Love does not remember, but cannot forget.
So death is not the answer, only an escape.
The old king gives her the perfect gift:
the moments of her own silence.
By this, she fulfills herself completely,
even beyond his love. What he knows
would not fit in the shell of a younger man.
He knows how to be nothing, how to die
easily, how to rise up again in the simple
reflection of all that she desires.

Sandstone House

John Joseph Mathews built the sandstone house
on his allotment, some five hundred acres of blackjacks
and red dirt. A stone house centered on a grand fireplace

not for warmth, but for the fire's cycles of life
reaching out to the prairie in all directions from its core.
I meet him passing through pages of old stories

about stray cattle, Arctic cold dropping in from the North,
and an old tree he can't cut down for its beauty. Symptoms of age
and sometimes, regret, strewn with a planetary melancholy,

an Oklahoma longing for a place as settled as those of his stones.
John moves back into the earth at a point where the wind
and the dry plains coalesce, and finds his place in weather

remembered in the cycles of life, the reason
he's returned. I see the sandstone house on his ridge as an eye
of the storm, where the land reaches up. He's its offering.

The house is not small but complete in a room, a space
that lends itself to the body. The inside like the outside,
not fully arranged. The windows are always open to wind.

The house sins only in its failed invisibility. He identifies
the trees that have outlasted the fires, outlasted the men, Osage,
who sat under them, who fought with the French against Washington,

outlasted the storms, the scavenging for fuel, all to this day
and are now dying. That was back in '45. And yet, here,
somehow, his space survives, his sandstone house flush with the sun.

III. When in Rome

"This Rome is the kingdom
of profitable payment. I arrived in April;
I am leaving in April. I have lost no time."

—C. P. Cavafy, "Alexandrian Merchant"

The Center of the Earth

On the Alentejo, in these hills
covered with sparse oak and olive,
the poor live out their days
in whitewashed cottages without light
or ready heat, or running water,
at the center of the Earth. Here,
where the Romans parsed out Europe,
divided up the regions among loyal
latifúndios, irrigated and grew
the first olive crops. Here, the Moors
brought rice and fruit, fought off
the Christian demands for land until
they too took flight. Here, the farmers
and shepherds returned to abandoned
churches, sheep straying into sacristies,
sleeping before the altars.
But the land retains its permanence
in oak, each decade strips bark
to cork the world's wine. Here, at last,
the Romans gave way to the Moors,
who gave way to the *Dom,*
and beneath them the land
haphazardly collected its seeds.
Europe's movements washed across
the Alto Alentejo, a matrix of desires,
invading peoples, displacing people,
to return the people finally, who
rise up quietly to take back the land.
Land remains the signature
of blood and marble, of olive oil,
cork, and wine, signed as all things
happen, all history, here like
everywhere, a center of the Earth.

The Writer and His Horse

Beside the table, out on the patio,
the laptop rests in a meditative stasis.

The horse chews a bolus in a field of dry grass,
its bell sounding a rhythm imposed on the day.

The writer hears only the horse's head swaying,
a signal for the shepherd if he strays further

than the breadth of this field. The patch of grass
eaten away, the horse stands momentarily to stare

into the writer's face. The bell ceases and
the day remains. The writer find his way.

Brennus and His Share of the Spoils (1893)

After the painting by Paul Jamin, "Le Brenn et sa part de butin"

In Jamin's eye, Brennus stands spread-legged in the doorway
surveying the chamber, which seems too small for his glory
but fits into the frame. The women huddled around the Apollo
are plumb, no matter what we may think today,

but they will not be that way for long. After all, who feeds
the slaves of the barbarian victors anyway?
Perhaps they will be used up in a day, for Brennus' prowess
is legendary. Or perhaps he's not so fond of women at all.

An old Roman warrior, hid half in the shadow of the door,
holds it open with two hands, trembling. The light behind the man
entering shows that history itself has set, in the way darkness
is now within the chamber, the empire's borders breached.

But none of this speaks to Paul Jamin in the late
Victorian age. When he thought about the glory of Rome
destroyed by the helterskelter hordes, and all the love
spilled out on that temple floor, he thought of Cezanne.

Four women naked, two tied, one in a last moment of despair
reaching up to the figure of Apollo, the golden god in miniature,
the dull metal moment when all the heavens fall to earth.
Naked spoils, the pinkish flesh of the girls.

Some jewels and fabrics are scattered in the corner,
but who cares? The painter knows the barbarian's soul,
as he knows Cezanne's bad eyes. Jamin, hungry for the moment
he has missed by two thousand years.

Popular Culture

It begins when I'm sitting still and ends in murder, so I switch it off.
Everything that remains disappears in quick chemical reactions, like love.
Then comes the blackout. In the dark, the body is all we have. As much
as possible, I avoid the politically correct names of things, or work
around them with pronouns. It is the most common here. We and you
evaporate like pools of standing water in the sun. No one can get beyond
the lingering side effects of the dominant culture. Bruises deep as the
bone. The dishpan hands, the dilated eyes, the reversals of history.
The self in a spotlight always melts. After all, it knows only the theater.
Each small new world of expectation flattens out beneath the weight
of desire. And yet, others fly around me, invincible in their skintight
red suits, lifting the shining word above their heads like a sword.
Why then is it so impossible to believe that the sentence must end?
What will archaeologists say when they discover the small doll in the
ruins that speaks in monosyllables and expresses the whole of cultural
history, limited only by our own time?

The Dogs of Yucatán

In memory of José Emilio Pacheco

The only way is to get down
on your knees and pray among them.
They are the community of the streets,

and all streets lead to sacrifice,
across the great plain of Aztec grief,
which is living, the other side

of evening. Across the lawns
of the Paseo de Montejo, the beasts
of the Avenue Reforma gather

for the night's prowl. Crossing
cautiously, the pools of water
where a clock of silver hangs,

five centuries carry them to a temple
many have forgotten. The dogs
do not bark. They have learned

their own sound is an enemy, an onslaught
of retribution. Death's still cheap,
and the sleeping kill in their sleep.

But the wealthy have moved to
other quarters. So the dogs
wake to roam the ancient

byways, searching for something
as yet unknown, something that
might sustain them: a scrap of leftover

civilization, a token someone dropped
on their way to the Underworld,
that will lead them back to Creation.

Hadrian's Wall

Of all these lives, the braided bits of experience
crisscross and rise like starlings

frightened from a door in the wall. The edge
of a New Jersey lawn, the world beyond.

Then older, the world no longer round but eggish,
it keeps its secrets in. Until you wander off the edge

into the realm of many-headed monsters
in four surrounding seas, as Cosmas Indicopleustes

rightly thought, for his time. Then, one night,
each star becomes a separate entity in your belief,

and darkness marks the limits of your empire.
Milecastles, fortlets, and Hadrian's Wall were knots

in a chain meant to keep the barbarians out.
But walls are made when separation is a fragile state,

and even then, some Pictish kin were dreaming me
beyond their own limits, the first expression

of an inner self. The walls cannot be breached.
They circle a world that has already been retrieved

from other worlds, and those from worlds before.
The wild Caledonians faded back beyond

the heather-an-dub walls of their Highlands,
to find that place you must look out of to see in.

After Celan

Only after, at the end
of the exam, after the table cleared
and the men departed, always men
mumbling words of congratulations,
almost awards, without naming the suspect,
this candidate succeeded in completing…

does Celan return to his home,
the birthright by grace of his
dead parents, to the space he inhabits
today, beyond the killing fields,
past the terror that he, as a poet,
was made to absorb.

I curve the word toward Iraq.
The ancient kingdom, invisible.
Words cured in the blood of biblical texts,
obscured by sand, ring out from
the dead. So much depends on
more than the text. That

was the difference he said, a German
could make, real feeling in steel,
like *absence,* and how it is played
off history. Forget family, friends,
the sudden deaths of so many others,
the final worth shifts to the future:
it is still unmade.

The Gates of Hell

Blind in Paris rain
that winter, I walked
straight into the Musée Rodin

by accident, as if
unknowingly in pursuit
of a presence, some stillness

I might stone within me,
or wear away at the edges
of time. Rodin's great

bronze gates poised
in an Edenic garden
strangely denature the nature

of his torment,
the mind's catalyst
for seeing *through* life.

Even late cast in bronze,
what we do seems suspect
in the end. An afternoon

spent catechizing
what there was to recover,
words spent.

Going someplace
that has no place,
the perfect relativity,

Rodin cures
with emptiness,
for thirty-seven years

pulling figures
from his Gate
to make images

in the larger life.
This way, surely,
through these gates,

borrowing his *revelation,*
fixed time, something
recast in the middle life,

unfinished, left hanging
on a plaster thread, the face
marooned in the mirror.

Men we could have been.
His *pièce de résistance*
now stationed

in an old wigmaker's garden
turned museum.
And at its head,

The Thinker, old Dante,
above in the tympanum,
suspended over his fist

like a weightlifter
preparing to hoist
the world.

The Fall of Rome

It was the slaves,
the prestige of *mancipia*,
running the city from beneath.

One time, there were a few
like houseplants, scattered
through our airy rooms.

Then came the games,
the fabulous moments of victory,
and all of the Palatine wanted them.

They overran the city
like hungry insects on a summer's day
swarming the dead streets.

In the servile wars, some say,
we grew fat with what we ate.
Others, that we opened

ourselves to desire,
and therefore defeat.
Having or not having is a city

divided by its only rule.
In the end, they are like us,
fat with pleasures,

satisfied to be taken care of,
to be needed if not loved,
but perfect in their poverty.

Romulus and Remus

Within each city, another sleeps.
Rising at dawn, a runner
greets it in the blood dark

there under the bridges
where the homeless build their homes
below Ponte Sant'Angelo.

Inside that darkness, another sleeps,
twin to the graffitists of Rome,
scrawling their quotes over the quotes

of Beckett, Wilde, and Joyce;
those who once visited Rome,
by those whose Rome it is.

Twin boys fed on lupus milk
harboring their hatreds
for each other.

Subterranean sleepwalkers
rising at dusk, and at dawn,
a parade of tourists,

their straw fedoras cocked,
their Hawaiian shirts untucked,
ordering cappuccinos *extra hot,*

and filling cafés
with a casual lust for the girls
walking to work.

But I suck on the teat of a she-wolf
to sustain this life
of a poet, the consul

who became a slave, the citizen
barbarian, the one who laughs
in the popes' crypt,

or at the spring slaughter
under umbrellas that prop up
the ruins of the Colosseum.

Saint Agnes, Outside

In a time of love,
when the body rests on rose petals,
rises from wine baths, or olive oil,
and the body is displayed
in every hallway, on every marble
pedestal, palace step, in every arena,
the body perfect in *contrapposto*,
figures loosely draped in *himatia*,
upright as gods, beyond reproach,
and all the Roman world lays
beyond the gates like a field
of lilies, she said no.

In a day when sex was
not an obligation, faceless
in its way, without frenzy
or neurosis, when to lie down
meant to live, then walk away,
born or bruised, but robbed
of nothing, when marriage
was *a situation,* and, worse,
to make love without payment,
outside of slavery, was *stupra,*
disloyalty, dishonor, a law
dealing death in its breech, then
honor too could be refusal.

So a basilica built on her aedicule,
built to complete the space
between love and sex, where she
waited for the Lord to take her out
of the brothels, and off the stake,
and perform the sacrificial fire
into saint, into untouchable, pre-
woman beyond the gaze of men,
and all at thirteen when it's said,

merely a maid, and the boys as
rude as sin, she told the pretty ones
to leave her alone, leave her
to her high bridal day, her body
but a coin in the well of her devotion.

IV. Illuminati

"Somewhere, everywhere, now hidden, now apparent in whatever
is written down, is the form of a human being."

—Virginia Woolf, "Reading"

Adagio for Pen and Song

For Gabriela Mistral

Asked her worth,
a poet trusts the first touch.
She sings Italian opera,
the French essence of desserts,
the names of extinct flowers,

the pace of the heart
on dacquoise, on tarte Tatin,
the Diminutive Powderpuff
and the Mace Pagoda
(remembered for being forgotten),

nothing worse. The poem
drops her name in the darkness
and she becomes the blood
flower again, her own
originary myth.

Back in time to the time
back of time, the poet trusts
the touch within, what everyone
wants: to be as good as
the image you preserve.

The Kennewick Man

"We will never be certain if his wound was by accident or intent, what language he spoke, or his religious beliefs. We cannot know if he is truly anyone's ancestor. Given the millennia since he lived, he may be sire to none or all of us."

—James C. Chatters

Dug out of soft mud
on Columbia riverbank,

a skull the size of a modern man's
transfigured by his pre-history.

Nine thousand years a blank slate,
stretched like skin to a face.

The lull in political activities
suggests an end to his history.

Dislodged from the muddy embrace
of postcolonial culture,

this skull by any other name
would smell as sweet.

The river's dance dresses and
undresses. The hosts and ghosts

say it is time for a burial.
But science wants a bit more.

Traces to family form
like the arthritis in his knee,

like the spear point in his thigh.
The causes of life's mysteries

have not changed. His blood is red,
a mark of migrations.

But these are the flaws
we find in everyone.

Dwelling

"We do not dwell because we have built, but we build and
have built because we dwell, that is, because we are dwellers."

—Martin Heidegger, *Poetry, Language, Thought*

Under overhanging cliffs, the self constructs its dwellings.
Living consumes the space we leave for it
like water down a narrow sandstone canyon; it builds

its kivas, its balconies, the single ladder that reaches to a secret
entrance and exit. No one believed the ruins would have this effect.
But a boy of twelve believes he haunts the spaces

of everything that has been. Ghosts are just pieces in the game.
When others speak of arid plains, of bluffs without access,
he pulls water from the myth of his own future.

But because their word is *ruin,* his early sense of culture
is rude as a park ranger's. After careless excavations,
he finds a truth in deer, in bighorn sheep, in how these others

help him to the fourth world. Between himself
and those who name the missing parts of history, he digs up
a shard of truth, a dampness beneath a stone, a storm way off

across the arid plain of his understanding. The yucca's thirst,
the wasp's evening flight, the coyote's high-pitched howl,
all are elements of his other self, the slickrock one,

the one who descends the ladder into the darkness of the kiva.
He finally learns to leave nothing that may fall
into the hands of looters, and climbs

the mesa to find the others making bricks of blood
and sandstone, using their breath for mortar, smoothing
the basin of the circular ruin, that will soon collect rain.

Ode to the Clay Army, Xi'an, China

Everyone comes here for the army
of the terracotta warriors, and then writes
poems. But I was not so impressed.
The soulless potteries of clay buried

in an underground city, forgotten
memory of a madman thinking this
might save his declining kingdom, the slaves
who must have labored into death

to build the imaginary. I'm more taken
with the old city walls, the fragmented
remains of odd corners, the gateway
passages gained by traffic now,

an empire deteriorating in the city's core.
The walls of this cell, years later,
are the same, fragments of master plans
that once sustained me

in the red brick heart of an urban madness.
The warriors would have been better
placed as curators of the already fallen,
as hollow clay guardians of a world

that one can only enter, and none leave,
when the memory vanishes suddenly,
when there are only buses
and tourists, and not enough time to eat,

before you are swept up into history,
mouths firmly sealed in hard defense,
the perfect at-attention, a city crumbling
around the tower of the self, stripped clean.

Chowder

The clams must come from heaven,
the milk, from the breasts of God.

Do not dice the little beasts but
coax them toward the final hour.

The miracle workers of the sea,
planktivorous eyelids of hunger, thriving

on the microscopic, skimmers, straining
the world through stone lips.

In the beginning, the onion was supreme,
perhaps for its many disguises, layer

upon layer of tears in the sea. Potatoes
believed they would never be eaten

for their simplicity, the earth's nuggets,
the silent eyeless witnesses of dirt.

And, of course, the *apogee of celery.*
But you stir them all slowly before me,

your arm in a whirlpool of time,
my eyes open wide to the moment

when you hesitate, wondering out loud,
will the world thicken enough

to sustain us? Are we buried beneath
a dream of sand, oceans rubbing

our backs? But love of the sea,
the creaturely pleasures of waves,

the moment just as the heat rises,
these are the makings of *chowda.*

The old way, before the briny catch
is completely clean, when love is a hunger.

The Barbarians

We talk each night along the quay
where the pizza parlors are stacked
as cards in a deck, waiting for the ships

to loll in, spend their single days
and cash, only to slip away into the dark
Mediterranean. A true Greek, I think,

until we settle in one evening, slow
time on the docks, the empty ocean
swallowing up the sounds of radios.

The proprietress admits she's Bulgarian,
some thirty years before, one of those
lost children of the world revolution,

escaping a Soviet zone, looking
for whatever could be bought without
a card. A barbarian, at the gates

of Rhodes, which stands behind us
in the half light, rises up
to tourist expectations.

We talk all night of collapsed
economies, and compare
the faces on our foreign coins.

Illuminati

For La Beata de Piedrahita,
there was a moment when she knew the irons of the Inquisition
might reach her. There was the darkness these men perpetuated,
she thought, and now I shall succumb. But among her patrons
and believers, she prized the fearful and a few with power
enough to keep her heresy from public eyes,
and to save her from the Tombs. But few knew
she'd spoken with the Virgin, and this was enough, she felt,
to secure her place wherever they might send her.

In Salamanca, in the household of her father,
who left each morning in his bondage to the builders,
labored for the Lord, in his way, by carrying stone
for the Church, she would wake to the suddenness of twilight
and not know if it were day at all, but perhaps some
filtered moment of her own forthcoming. Still as
the small house was with her father gone,
it was a sentence she knew she must live with.
She felt the worlds rub close together and nothing
more for this one could be done.

It was not the forms of darkness, the *alumbrados*
and their Gnostic sources, but those others, hidden
for what must have seemed forever, who found
in her voice the bridge to God's syllables, a light of itself
splendiferous, congealing. She held council with the Lord
they told their judges, and so would know the ends of these inquiries
into the true faith. She would have given herself up
to whatever forces, for they were small, and limited to
the temporal. While others burned, and few, at the instant
of the fire, would say more than that they *corresponded,*
she reached for the light, ambered in the flames.

The South Cross

Monasterboice, Boyne Valley, Ireland

Half the cross is archaeology.
But the need to know spurred
the carvers on, no doubt,
faith in their own strength,
lifting hammer to heaven
to hit chisel to unyielding stone.

If the fifteen-meter High cross
seems somehow at odds with disbelief,
backtrack to the time when science
mixed in magic. The poet's passion
in monk or abbot, words rough-hewed
into the surface of the mind.

We find the human love
of the fantastic. The Celts drawn
to David all night in the lion's den,
to St. Peter in his fight with Simon,
the flying magician, who's brought
crashing down into the earth.

Ecce Homo. And only human.
What more could be scripted?
Warrior king with ring-head crown,
arms outstretched like the sun god
that precedes him. He translates well.
Faith is the swing and arc of a hammer.

Saint Agnes Returns to Rome

She's so small, she fits
in a demitasse, white swimmer
in the dark extremes,
in espresso bliss
before clouds dissolve
and everyone returns
to work.

She has a moped, a tiny
scooter that skirts the issues
of deadly Mercedes, of robes
and turbans, skinheads,
pitch-perfect itinerant scenes,
skirts the walls
to find her way to markets
of fresh flowers.

Sex today is a washing machine
someone says to her—
she is thirteen—you throw
everything in and swirl it
around an urban paradise
of ramshackle, brokedown
apartment blocks just
beyond the Vatican.

The statues in St. Peter's
are of old men, earth gray,
collecting cell phone flashes
in low light, creating a post-
modern apocalypse,
lie down with me,
end of the world.

Agnes pulls her raw sweater on,
stands before a third floor
window, dreaming of a boy
who wanted her once,
who she refused, banished,
waiting now for a god
to pick her up at noon.

Schoenberg's Daughter's White Cat

On a grainy, California coast,
in those years just before the War
blotted out memory, making real
the mean little differences

of culture, Schoenberg's daughter
appears on the film more central than he,
proudly chasing her cat.
The sun-state day is obviously hot.

The world waits. And while above her
the adults argue and complain
(perhaps of the coming destruction),
she wanders down the stairs

fully aware of nothing
but the elusive whiteness of her feline mate
and the warmth of her summer's day,
and perhaps her father's madness.

The Unseen

For Steven and Syl

I did not know her well
but watched you give up
the hard currency of your life

to countermand the comets
of her errant limbs, the sad
smiles that would sprout

out of the slender hour
under your partial hold.
As if the world were good

enough, or good in passing,
not overwrought with grief
or the self-pitying we find

in the dictates of forgiveness,
you cut clean to the bone
without a knife or symbol

or doctrine. When her fingers
curled into night-triggered buds
and she could not walk

a straight line, you held
tight to the body you loved,
like she were the raft against

your drowning. Even so, as
others gathered to talk
of her strength in surviving,

it was clear you'd survived
a different flood, and now had
only a long swim to shore.

Belled Horses in a Portuguese Field

Some places, the world stops for sounds. The horses
drifting through the high grass like ships, the shush

of a month in spring spent writing in their green harbor.
They've come to stand at the edge of my deck

lined in temporary stones a thousand years old,
Roman bricks from a buried farm. The proprietor here

cut a path, uncircumspect, and unearthed a grange
from the time of the first push against the Celts.

I hear unsettled voices in the citrus groves and olive orchards,
against the sound of hand axes cutting through the porous

skins of oak that will cork bottles of Madeira and Tejo,
against the fine ting of glasses set out in the evening

in a reddening transparency of hills and fields
where the horses' bells ring through the veil like anchors,

clanging their riff in the day's false flourishes
that stumble out onto this soundless page.

Phoenicians, Greeks, and Carthaginians, all here,
quiet in the blood. Their memory cannot jibe with now

for it lacks the immediacy of sounds. I hear before
I think, the hand-wrought iron of the horses' bells,

but the Greeks also believed in the gift of silence,
and a poet who springs from the belly of a horse.

Capela Dos Ossos

> "By the 16th century, there were as many as 43 cemeteries in and around Évora that were taking up valuable land. Not wanting to condemn the souls of the people buried there, the monks decided to build the Chapel and relocate the bones."

> —*Atlas Obscura,* The Chapel of Bones, Évora, Portugal

If the truth was somehow
beyond death, dying was yet
a sign of it. The monks

were plain: keep the worms
in mind. Later came
the architecture. A chapel

built of bones to visualize
a universe of what is left,
life as *memento mori.*

Whatever you do, do not
presume. The grotto echoes
like a sea washing creatures

free of the rocks. Bones grow
light with time, remains
are more like paper,

a palimpsest of scripts,
or nameless entries
in the book of days.

The skulls have a way
of staring at you. Notice
how the darkness sings?

The chapel roughs the edge
of night, brings out
the other side of things.

What remains? Ego in
a bone cage. Monks unburied
that sacred sense of now.

Birds of the Alentejo

On the high plateau of Portugal,
the pigs scrounge out all
the grass and bark,

bend the small trees down
with the weight of their hunger.
But the birds go on chattering

an Alentejo tic among
these other species. Names
escaping are of little importance.

These are human things:
the way we have of feeling
not quite alone.

The birds speak a different tongue
of pure desire. A deeper need
to find, to eat,

that is not like the pig's voracity,
a hunger of the air.
Open to other possibilities,

they do not rest on their stomachs.
The birds enjoy a singling out
of time in the morning hours,

a swirl of separateness,
trill to low call. But caught
in the cacophony,

who can eat or sleep?
I'm only another listener,
but the birds make clear

the difference. All that has
occurred, all that time consumes,
in a moment, disappears.

V. Extinctions

"I want to stand as close to the edge as I can without going over.
Out on the edge you see all the kinds of things you
can't see from the center."

—Kurt Vonnegut

Spanish Grave

A small cairn of stones
off the coast of Skagaströnd,
Iceland, on a thumb of land

that juts proudly
into the North Sea.
A Viking death,

or some Viking slave,
now an unmarked grave.
The sign says simply

spænska dys. Nearby
columnar jointings
of basalt make

long nails
on a black hand
of coastal stone.

So geologic
time countermands
cardinal death,

natural monuments
displace old sympathies,
and we are more fascinated

by hexagonal shapes
than by a foreigner's death
in a foreign age.

The sea crystallizes
when it meets molten rock,
forming colonnades

and entablatures,
which seem to bend
in the Northern Wind,

making earth's
catastrophes unequaled
and untranslatable.

Between Christmas and New Year's

"Between Christmas and New Year's 2006, five U.S. soldiers committed suicide upon being informed they'd been ordered to serve an additional tour in Iraq."

—Robin Morgan, from *The Humanist*

In the field, the newly fallen.
But it is not a field any longer but sand in waves

and the five dead are celebrating Christmas
with Christ, with the darkness, who

can be sure? Each grain of sand is its own
element of the universe, formed out of desire,

the Big Bang, and recalls Father Arnall's sermon
and Joyce's metaphors for Hell, for time,

a way of speaking, two things
unrelated, two things that have one purpose

beyond meaning. A bird carries away a grain of sand
each million years, one grain off a mountain

a million miles high. Eternity. One life
at a time, one year at Christmas and the time made

to forget, when days once shortened by the sun's increase,
pœna damni, the pain of loss, finds its measure. IEDs

are revelatory, enemies, invisible brethren, whatever
we believe, belief itself becomes a doubtful silence,

the unnatural thing, celebration confused, as when
Claudius claims a mirth in funeral. . .a defeated joy.

The random season, a love that cannot save a feeling
that death eradicates, does not make up

for sacrifice, as words might only feign a greeting.
There are men dead and are we the cause, or

is it the cause that kills them? Between forgetting
and New Year's, lives are spent, passages resumed,

and we amend the numbers
by the division of our prayers,

for each is a particle of sand the bird carries
across the desert we must call home.

How the World Works in Iceland

Here the rains bring down dark carbons crashing
into basalt rock, and there they cling to calcium, carried
in new form, broken down, to the bottom of the sea,

and the air, not clean but cleaning, the slate gray world
churns, a factory in reverse, sucking in otherworldly coal
emissions and coughing out dead chemicals,

limestone rebirth, to recombine with earth. Beneath the streets
of Reykjavik, the thermal heat streams down from the hills
without electricity, without fuel burning air,

and bacteria eat the sulphide from geothermal steam beds
before our carbons blacken the sun, and so the darkness
we have started comes full circle to the light,

and barren rock and primal creature life
take back our mistakes, breaking up the poison wastes,
on a simple island floating gently in the palm of the earth.

The Caper Berry

The bud the tongue
cannot tell from its flower,
green as the little river on Paros,
an undiscovered thread
through the village
of Lefkes.

But greener still,
this love brewing in
the butcher shop. You,
the light wine of my time,
sunlight inside, sudden, alive.
Bud on the end of my tongue.

The Elgin Marbles

"The sea-ruling Britannia snatched the last spoils
of Greece, that was in the throes of death."

—Lord Byron

As with other famous crimes in history,
the marbles were given the thief's name,

and shipped away to stand in a dirt shack
before the old Lord's drunken friends.

But the horses are angry! Look at the snouts!
Athena's pageants stripped away,

centuries of shame in the roofless sun,
centuries of the Church and Ottomans,

and the walls fall to the morality of new men.
Today, in the economics of collapse,

the horses rear their heads above
the European fray. They stomp and snort,

and it's said one hoof came down
on the thief's weak heart, and years later

carried him away. So the museum houses
Cavafy's curse, and the older, Eleusinian one.

Extinctions

No managing of myths
can make them solely female.
Wolves pair, they split, they
couple as elements do in
the fury of nuclear fusion.
Their bad name made scavenger,
pack-deaths, their hunger reviled,
we forget their culling of herds
or that highbred consciousness
as movement out of endangered
territories. A hundred and twenty-five
miles in a day. We mark
highways with less magnitude.
Down from the north
where the hole through
the middle of the Earth
carries our ideas
of 19th-century ocean currents,
they pass through, Arctic
to Gray wolf, Red wolf
to Mexico, barely disturbed
except by the mingling
of our extinctions.

Lightning

It's alright now to speak of it. The bluish-white crack
rattling the sky, the sudden displacement of air molecules

that dance, clap, then rip, a blast of earth built up to waken
the gods. It's alright now, for you're not with me, watching,

but off somewhere where only sheet lightning blares
and cannot really sign its name, reaching every which way

but down, never writing its signature on the eye. The rush
of ionized air, the taste of fear that dances its death dance

along the wire, drawn up from the passive ground. The positive
universe splits open, subsides, the clouds laugh out loud.

That's what we witnessed, the moment fissured in two, forked
toward the devils in the earth, the sudden skin of our two lives

itching to speak in galvanized words. You'd known an eastern
muted light, only the rumbling of shaken-out sheets,

and this was our first shared immediacy. The ladder to the earth,
up which our imaginations climbed, quickly, like spikes of light,

or lacerations in the canopy, highlighting low clouds cast out,
stricken, feeling earth kiss sky in bright, frozen time.

Why We Work with Our Hands

For Fred

Because they are sympathetic with the wood
and know the purity of its frozen rivers, the red
that does not bleed, the white sapwood that slows
even as the seasons slow, their mazy grains,
their longevity, the way trees never move
and move continuously.

Because hands are the light creatures
who live at the outposts of our bodies, these
ministers to the world's savageries,
that touch the wood as if it were alive, knowing
how it grew in our absence, within the silent copse,
under the pleasure of a dark canopy.

The board balances on the dead planks of its horse
and the wood smells sweet with a residue of its love,
aroused, as it should be, for we know wood
as our bodies know lovers, by the grain and sinew
of their masks. The chair made by a man who died
goes to auction and the hands forget.

Chairs suffer haphazard swings and bruises of disuse.
But the wood remembers, in its slowing labyrinth
of the last monsoon, the felling, the rings that harden
into histories, into fingerprints that foretell
the hand's return. So when the wood is soaked
and bent to hoop, rain gathers in its barrels

or sails carry it out to mount a last resistance
on the sea. Or men take it up and nail together
the frames of houses, feeling at once its
lightness and surrender, knowing that dust
in time settles like moth silk on its eyes, and rain
again will ratoon its limbs with crucifixions.

The Butcher's Table

In workshop, we read
pleasant things about flowers
dipped in blood, or horses
with their heads cut off,
or the odd divorce, silently
circling like a winter hawk.

And when we're done,
the butcher comes and cuts meat
on our table, his table, cuts
thick thighs of pork and
shoulders of beef, and makes
our poems into bloodless

dreams, echoes of anger
and disbelief. Each swing
of his arm like the falling
of a sword, each sigh in his
daily work, the sound of a poem
escaping into the world.

Acknowledgments

I would like to thank the following journals in which some of these poems first appeared:

About Place Journal: "Dwelling"
Allegro: "The Kennewick Man"
American Poetry Abroad: "Spanish Grave"
Ante Review: "The Unexpected Nature of Things"
Arbutus: "Of Two Pietás"
Arc: "Waiting Room"
Ascent Aspirations: "A Skull on Orkney" (as "Skull")
The Big Toe: "Between Christmas and New Year's"
Blue Bear Review: "After Cavafy"
Blue Fifth Review: "Popular Culture"
The Centrifugal Eye: "The Center of the Earth"
Compose: "Birds of the Alentejo"
Copaiba Quarterly: "The Elgin Marbles"
Curio: "A Wild Grave"
Danse Macabre: "The Butcher's Table," "The Death of Modernism"
Dante's Heart: "Extinctions"
Diode: "Brennus and His Share of the Spoils (1893)," "After Celan,"
    "Note Saves Me from Despair"
Drafthorse: "Why We Work with Our Hands"
Empty Mirror: "The Order of Things"
Five Poetry Magazine: "The Writer and His Horse"
Furnace Review: "The Barbarians"
Green Door (Flanders): "Translating Cavafy"
Hobble Creek Review: "The South Cross"
Ink Bean: "Café on the Alentejo"
Innisfree Poetry Journal: "How to Handle a Rattlesnake"
IthacaLit: "Capela dos Ossos, Évora, Portugal," "Lightning," "Chowder"
Magma: "How the World Works in Iceland"
Mud Season Review: "Boat to Skellig Michael," "Schoenberg's Daughter's
    White Cat"
Osiris: "Icelandic Time," "Gentle to Violent Rain," "At Skibbereen,"
    "Belled Horses in a Portuguese Field"
Passionate Transitory: "The Dogs of Yucatán"
Poetry Bay: "Spanish for Tourists"
Prairie Poetry: "Sandstone House"
Queen's Quarterly: "The Swim to Iceland"
Scythe: "Ode to the Clay Army, Xi'an, China"

SNR Review: "Illuminati"
St. Petersburg Review: "Hadrian's Wall"
The 13th Warrior: "The Unseen"
Tipton Poetry Review: "The Caper Berry"
Valparaiso: "Saint Agnes Outside the Walls"

C. P. Cavafy, "Alexandrian Merchant," is quoted from *The Complete Poems of Cavafy* (Harcourt Brace & Co., 1976). Translated by Rae Dalven.

Cover artwork, "Birds and Cross" by George Moore; author photo by Tammy Moore; cover and interior book design by Diane Kistner; Centaur MT Pro text and titling

About FutureCycle Press

FutureCycle Press is dedicated to publishing lasting poetry books, chapbooks, and anthologies in the English language, in both print-on-demand and Kindle ebook formats. Founded in 2007 by long-time independent editor/publishers and partners Diane Kistner and Robert S. King, the press incorporated as a nonprofit in 2012. A number of our editors are distinguished poets and writers in their own right, and we have been actively involved in the small press movement going back to the early seventies.

The FutureCycle Poetry Book Prize and honorarium is awarded annually for the best full-length volume of poetry we publish in a calendar year. Introduced in 2013, our Good Works projects are anthologies devoted to issues of universal significance as well as other efforts in support of poets and writers—with all proceeds donated to a related worthy cause. Our Selected Poems series highlights contemporary poets with a substantial body of work to their credit; with this series we strive to resurrect work that has had limited distribution and is now out of print.

We are dedicated to giving all of the authors we publish the care their work deserves, making our catalog of titles the most diverse and distinguished it can be, and paying forward any earnings to fund more great books.

We've learned a few things about independent publishing over the years. We've also evolved a unique, resilient publishing model that allows us to focus mainly on vetting and preserving for posterity poetry collections of exceptional quality without becoming overwhelmed with bookkeeping and mailing, fundraising activities, or taxing editorial and production "bubbles." To find out more about what we are doing, come see us at www.futurecycle.org.

The FutureCycle Poetry Book Prize

All full-length volumes of poetry published by FutureCycle Press in a given calendar year are considered for the annual FutureCycle Poetry Book Prize. This allows us to consider each submission on its own merits, outside of the context of a contest. Too, the judges see the finished book, which will have benefitted from the beautiful book design and strong editorial gloss we are famous for.

The book ranked the best in judging is announced as the prize-winner in the subsequent year. There is no fixed monetary award; instead, the winning poet receives an honorarium of 20% of the total net royalties from all poetry books and chapbooks the press sold online in the year the winning book was published. The winner is also accorded the honor of being on the panel of judges for the next year's competition; the judges receive copies of all contending books to keep for their personal libraries.

www.ingramcontent.com/pod-product-compliance
Lightning Source LLC
Chambersburg PA
CBHW070008100426
42741CB00012B/3159